*Dedicated to you, child.
May you forever feel
the wonders of Christmas
and the joy of generosity —
especially now that you are learning
The World's Best-Kept Secret.*

Let's talk about Santa.

Have you been
wondering about him?

That's okay.
Most of us do.

This book will help
answer your questions.

Are you ready?

Dear Santa,
How do you travel around the whole world in one night?

Here's a big question you might be asking a lot lately.

How can Santa's magical, generous gift giving around the *entire* world in *one* night even be possible?

Okay. Time for the answer.
(It's big.)
Ready, set... rotate the book.

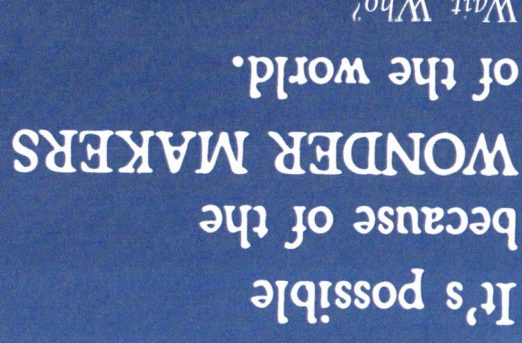

It's possible
because of the
WONDER MAKERS
of the world.

Wait. Who?
That's another great question.

YOUR PARENTS ARE THE WONDER MAKERS.

That's right. Moms and dads — and sometimes even grandparents and big brothers and sisters — all work together to create the magic of Christmas morning.

But... what about Santa?

Yes, there really *was* a Santa.
Sort of. Well, not exactly.

The truth is, today's Wonder Makers are inspired by the generosity of a man named Nicholas. He lived a long, long time before you were born — almost two thousand years ago — in a land now called Turkey.

We like to say Nicholas was the *original* Santa. However, *Santa* wasn't his actual name. (Dutch families called him "Sinter Klaas," which evolved into "Santa Claus.") And while he didn't fly from country to country on eight tiny reindeer, he *did* do some remarkable things.

Nicholas brought wonder and joy to the world by giving surprise gifts to people living in nearby villages. It is said that he often delivered these gifts secretly at night while traveling upon a white horse, quietly placing the gifts inside families' windows.

Nicholas devoted his life to helping others. For his countless good deeds, he became known as "Saint Nicholas the Wonderworker."

Long after Nicholas died, his legacy spread around the world. People yearned for the wonder and joy he had given others. So in the early 1800s, they decided to keep it going.

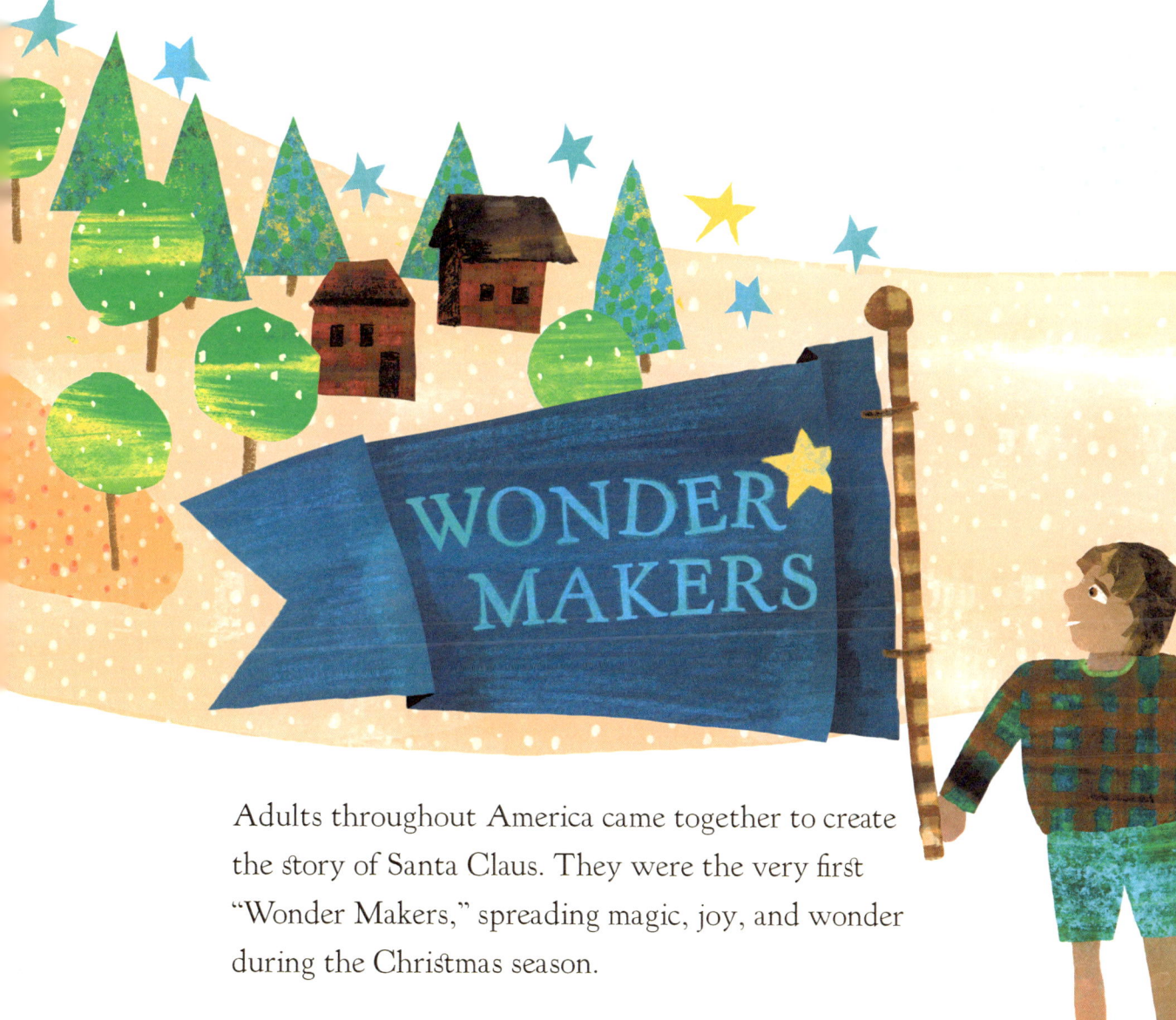

Adults throughout America came together to create the story of Santa Claus. They were the very first "Wonder Makers," spreading magic, joy, and wonder during the Christmas season.

THE WORLD'S BEST-KEPT SECRET IS THIS

People who love you and wish for you to feel joy and wonder during the Christmas season have been giving you secret gifts "from Santa."

No, the world does not have a real Santa Claus flying through the night sky magically delivering gifts to every boy and girl.

But we *do* have adults and big kids (our Wonder Makers) who have worked for hundreds and hundreds of years to keep the secret of Santa alive. And *that* in itself is quite magical!

Some secrets are meant for good. Others aren't.

Our Santa Claus Secret is meant to be a GOOD secret. SHHH

The Wonder Makers keep the good secret
for as long as they can because of the joy it
brings young boys and girls to experience the
wonder of Santa Claus, just as you have.

And now you know the secret too.

Maybe you had a hunch already.

Maybe you're feeling sad or confused now.
Many of us do at first. That's okay.

Hi!
Congrats on being part of the big Christmas secret-keeper squad! When I first learned the truth, I felt as if Christmas would never be the same. Turns out, Christmas is still so much fun! It is especially fun if you're like me and can keep the magic alive by helping surprise your younger sister during the holidays. Seeing how excited she gets makes my day 10x better. Plus, getting presents isn't too bad either, Ha Ha! Cherish every moment of it!

Maya

Hey new kid. Ok so here's the thing — the secret. Every year, our moms and dads filled our stockings and chose and wrapped our presents, and put them under the tree — just like their parents did for them, and just like we probably will for our own kids someday! Kinda crazy, right?

Welcome to the club.

Hey you! Now YOU know the secret!

So now you know too! Make sure to help your 'Santas' and remember to stay quiet.
— Eric

Hi!
I found out about the big secret at the same time as my brother. We were both worried that the magic of Christmas would be gone.

But, don't worry! Christmas is still just as magical and special, and it is still my favorite holiday! I love when "Santa" visits my grandparents' house and being able to watch the joy it brings to my little cousins! We use jingle bells to sound like his sleigh! It is a fun secret to be a part of!

—Tori

Let's GO! :) Nolan

I know you're probably surprised or upset, or maybe you've known this whole time and didn't know how to tell your parents! It's ok! ☆

Keep the secret for us please. You wouldn't want to be the one who brings another kid down!

Love ya ♡ —Ella

What does this all mean for YOU?

Well, it's pretty special.

It means that someone who loves you is a Wonder Maker. You might even have *a few* Wonder Makers in your life.

Your Wonder Makers have thoughtfully gathered the gifts you have received "from Santa" each Christmas.

Your Wonder Makers have wished for you to feel joy, warmth, and wonder every time you have gazed upon the gifts that mysteriously arrived after you went to sleep on Christmas Eve.

And most of all, now that you know this secret, your Wonder Makers hope for you to feel this joy, warmth, and wonder *forever*.

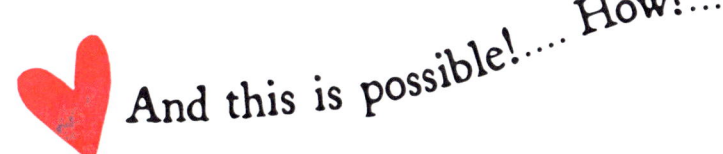 And this is possible!..... How?...

.......How?.........All you have to do is be a part of the wonder.

WONDER MAKER'S PROMISE

Starting today, it's your turn.

You now know The World's Best-Kept Secret.

And it's up to you to keep it.

Are you ready to be a Wonder Maker, too?

 I understand that the wonder and spirit of the "Santa Story" is still alive today, and I want to be a part of making it happen for others.

Your Signature

 I will keep the World's Best-Kept Secret to myself (and with fellow Wonder Makers like my parents). I will never take away someone else's opportunity to experience the wonder of Santa.

Your Signature

 I will spread kindness and joy just as Saint Nicholas did centuries ago. It's my turn to think of others and give generously — and sometimes secretly — without expecting anything in return.

Your Signature

 I promise to keep the wonderfulness of Christmas in my heart, always.

Your Signature

Do you promise to fulfill the duties of a Wonder Maker? Sign your name on the dotted lines and begin your journey.

WONDER-MAKING IDEAS

Ready to be a part of the Wonder?
Here are a few ideas you could try this year.

★ SECRETLY give something thoughtful and UNEXPECTED to someone like my neighbor, my teacher, or my friend. I won't reveal that it's from me!

★ Pick out a special gift for my little brother, sister, or cousin, and help HIDE it under the Christmas tree.

 Take a bite out of Santa's cookies this Christmas Eve before bed to help my parents out.
Or make reindeer hoofprints on the driveway!

 yum.

⭐ BE JOYFUL ☺ when I see a Santa in public, and when people talk or sing about Santa. ♪

⭐ Oooh! One more ↓

When you get older, you'll have even more opportunities to be a Wonder Maker for those you love.

What's Your Idea?

Enjoy keeping the secret and sharing the wonder of Christmas!

A NOTE ABOUT THE AUTHORS

A few eager Wonder Makers wrote this book for you, but there are Wonder Makers everywhere — in homes all over the world. Most don't consider themselves Wonder Makers. They probably just call themselves Dad, Mom, Brother, Sister, Grandma, or Grandpa. It's not a term that's widely-used… but it will be, if you continue the tradition.

Long live the Wonder Makers!

WONDER MAKER
★ MEMORY KEEPER

On this day: _____
I officially learned the World's Best-Kept Secret.

All the ways I'm feeling right now:

 ☐ EXCITED  ☐ SAD ☐ ANGRY  ☐ HAPPY  ☐ SHY   ☐ SILLY ☐ PROUD  ☐ TIRED

 ☐ WORRIED  ☐ LOVED  ☐ ANNOYED   ☐ EMBARRASSED  ☐ SCARED  ☐ DISAPPOINTED ☐ CONFUSED  ☐ BORED

Who else in my family knows the big secret?

Who in my family *doesn't* know yet?

Some of my favorite **gifts** from "Santa" have been:

One of my most-loved Christmas **memories** is:

Something I'm **looking forward** to this Christmas:

One thing I'm **wishing** for this Christmas:

AFTERWORD
More About The Secret, Santa, and Saint Nicholas

MORE ABOUT THE SECRET

Learning this big secret — our so-called World's Best-Kept Secret — can be difficult. We grow up believing Santa lives in our world doing wonderful things, and then one day, we discover there is no magical Santa flying through the sky on reindeer, and our parents and loved ones have been doing these wonderful things instead!

What's helpful to recognize during this discovery is that *there still is wonder and joy in the story of Santa*. In fact, when we look back to the centuries-old origin story of Santa Claus in America, we see that this secret was born from a desire to bring warmth and good cheer to a holiday that had become primarily adult-oriented. Inspired by the Dutch tradition of celebrating Saint Nicholas and our yearning to bring joy into the homes of young children, we created the idea of Santa Claus, and we as a society have **wonderfully managed to keep the secret alive generation after generation.**

MORE ABOUT SANTA

If we could peer into the homes and halls of 17th- and 18th-century America, we would see the Christmas holiday being celebrated mainly by adults with festivities like banquets and ball dancing, with no signs of children or secret gifts waiting beneath trees. It wasn't until the early 1800s that a few

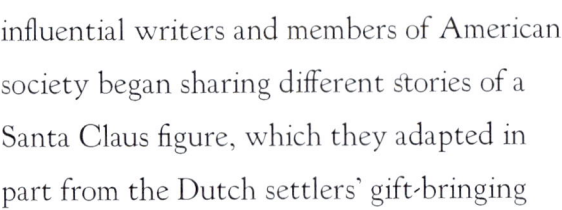

influential writers and members of American society began sharing different stories of a Santa Claus figure, which they adapted in part from the Dutch settlers' gift-bringing tradition of celebrating Saint Nicholas ("Sinterklass").

America's introduction of Santa Claus brought a new focus on children and families and transformed the Christmas holiday into a time of good cheer and gift-giving within the home. Parents and children bonded in the folklore as the season became more magical in anticipation and wonderment of what gifts were going to be delivered by Santa Claus.

Our 19th-century Santa story caught on because it lit up the hearts and minds of adults and children alike. And our so-called Wonder Makers were beautifully orchestrating every surprise and delight of Santa's visits. We as a society yearned for the joy of Santa, and we made it happen — essentially, and eventually — worldwide.

MORE ABOUT SAINT NICHOLAS

Although Saint Nicholas was the most celebrated saint in European history for centuries, he himself had nothing to do with the Christian-based Christmas story as it is told today. Dutch families celebrated Saint Nicholas on December 6th, the anniversary of his death, by surprising children with presents left secretly in their shoes "by Saint Nicholas," as their story went. His feast day being so close to the Christmas holiday is likely how he became the muse of today's Santa Claus.

Saint Nicholas was born around 280 A.D. in what is now Turkey and was orphaned as a young boy. It is said that he gave away all of the wealth inherited from his parents and traveled the countryside helping children in need, struggling families, and the ill.

Through the centuries many stories and legends have been told of St. Nicholas' life and good deeds. Today we don't know which of these stories are true (or not), but we do know he was a man whose life was filled with an abundance of generosity.

The World's Best-Kept Secret | Copyright © 2023 by Orange Magnets LLC
All rights reserved. This book, or parts thereof, may not be reproduced in any form without written permission in writing from the publisher and author.
Orange Magnets Books | orangemagnets.com | ISBN 979-8-9895259-0-4 (hardback edition)

Written and Illustrated by Michelle Hanke, who wishes to thank her fellow Wonder Maker, Curt Hanke, for his creative and editorial expertise in the making of this book.

www.ingramcontent.com/pod-product-compliance
Lightning Source LLC
Chambersburg PA
CBRC091212010526
44119CB00021B/376